ABOVE
A vibrant display of poppies outside one of
the lovely manor houses in the Cotswolds.

PREVIOUS PAGES
Hadrian's Wall, Northumberland, was built by the
Emperor Hadrian in AD 122 as a defence
against Pictish invaders.

OVERLEAF
The village of Ashwellthorpe is set in the heart
of Norfolk's pastoral countryside.

FACING FOREWORD
A Yeoman Warder at the Tower of London

BACK ENDPAPER
The Brigade of Guards take part in Trooping
the Colour, on the Queen's Official Birthday.

Colourful
BRITAIN

FOREWORD *by Lord Montagu of Beaulieu*

I am delighted to be associated with this beautiful new book on Britain. All over the world the townscapes and landscapes are changing very fast – for some too fast – but in Britain we are proud that a great deal of care and devotion is continuously lavished on conserving our heritage and making it available for the public to see.

Britain has been a nation of seafarers, explorers and colonisers, and its past wealth was the result of the prestigious efforts and enterprise of our ancestors. Our houses, both great and small, were built by men who were able to employ all the best talent of the period and fill them with artistic treasures from the world over. Their upkeep, as I know from personal experience, is very costly and every year becomes more so, but the historic houses of Britain are unique in the world, insomuch as they are still homes and not museums, and they are able to survive because of the increasing number of tourists who are attracted to them. For years now it has been my particular concern to gain official recognition of the needs of these surviving monuments to our past history and the Government and the public of this country are now fully aware of the extent of the problems.

Apart from its buildings, Britain is also blessed with a varied and beautiful countryside. The mountains and valleys of Wales on its west coast change gradually to the flat, fertile fens of the east, while Scotland to the north is a land of mountains with great lochs, many having their own mysterious legend. The New Forest, where I live, is virgin countryside, untouched by the plough for 900 years and still harbouring four species of deer.

The British people are as diverse as their landscape. Many of the Welsh still retain their own Celtic language and universal education has not dimmed the interest and charm of regional accents and dialects.

The great tourist centres of London, Winchester, York, Stratford, Bath, Chester, Canterbury and Edinburgh, to name only a few, annually attract many tourists but it is often away from these more popular places that the greatest pleasure and interest is to be found. Britain has a long history with a culture that goes back to Roman times, and remains of this past are often to be discovered in out-of-the-way places. There is hardly a country in the world which has not some connection with Britain, especially the vast English-speaking world, so many of whom still look upon Britain as the mother country and also share with Britain its language, literature and customs.

May I wish all lovers of beauty a happy and rewarding time exploring our island and, especially if you come from overseas, may I hope that you will take back precious memories of our own land and return again and again. You will always be most welcome.

February 1980

In 1951 Lord Montagu, the third Baron of Beaulieu, inherited the Beaulieu Manor Estate in Hampshire and opened his home, Palace House, to the public.

In the grounds of the house he founded the Montagu Motor Museum which, in 1972, became the now world-famous National Motor Museum. This museum houses a unique collection of vintage cars, bicycles and motorcycles and these exhibits, along with the Reference and Photographic Libraries, and Palace House and the ruins of the early thirteenth-century Beaulieu Abbey, attract approximately 600,000 visitors a year.

Lord Montagu was appointed the first President of the Historic Houses Association and he is now the President of the European Union of Historic Houses as well as the President of the Southern Tourist Board. The many duties attached to these posts involve frequent travelling abroad and Lord Montagu is an enthusiastic ambassador for the many attractions of Great Britain. He has done much to promote the cause of British tourism abroad, particularly in North America.

INTRODUCTION

Britain is an island in which over the centuries many different races have learnt to live together in peace and co-operation. Until some 9,000 years ago Britain was a part of the continent of Europe, but very little is known of its earliest inhabitants. Agricultural communities began to establish themselves some 3,000 years before the Roman occupation in AD 43. They have left many fascinating memorials to their culture, by far the most spectacular being Stonehenge in Wiltshire. Built 1800 BC, it is the finest example of a Bronze Age sanctuary in Europe. Hill-top forts, megalithic burial tombs and round barrows also abound, the largest and most mysterious being Silbury Hill, also in Wiltshire. A considerable amount of trading was conducted with the outside world, mostly in tin, a product of the Cornish tin mines, and thus a flourishing export trade was established long before the Romans conquered Britain and made it a part of the Roman Empire.

Despite fierce opposition, the disciplined Roman legions quickly overcame local resistance and for four centuries Britain was a Roman outpost. The Romans brought great changes in their wake. A fine system of roads was built which provided the nucleus of our major inter-city routes until the new motorways came into being after the last war, giving us for the first time a logical plan based upon modern needs. In order to combat the incursions of the so-called barbarians in the North, the Romans built a great wall of some seventy miles' length, parts of which survive to this day, the best example being at Housesteads in Northumbria. This great wall with its regular system of forts was garrisoned for over 200 years and was not abandoned until the year AD 383. This was the time when, because of needs elsewhere, the Roman legions were gradually withdrawn from Britain and it marked the end of Roman rule and the beginning of a new phase in British history – the gradual occupation of the country by Anglo-Saxon invaders who settled in what is now England, driving the original inhabitants into Wales and Cornwall.

Christianity was introduced to Britain in the latter part of the sixth century by St Augustine. This new religion soon replaced the fierce gods of the Anglo-Saxons and brought literacy to the land through those sanctuaries of learning, the monasteries, and Britain settled to a period of peace and development. The Danish invasion in the ninth century brought a rude end to this peace and once more war and pillage was rife in the land.

Much of what happened in the next four centuries is shrouded in myth and legend. These were the 'Dark Ages' during which the Church struggled to keep alive the learning and culture imported from Europe. Probably the most significant date in British history was 1066. In that year William of Normandy, at the head of an invading army, fought a famous battle at Hastings, defeating the Saxons under Harold. The successful Normans, landowners and aristocrats, imposed their rule on the Saxon peasantry although life at the lower level went on practically unchanged. The hatred of the Norman masters by the Saxons is shown in the legendary characters of Robin Hood and Hereward the Wake, two Saxon heroes who still capture the imagination of the English people today. The England of those days would have been a land of great forests filled with deer and wild boar. Small timber settlements would have clustered around the local strongposts or castles. Monasteries, often possessing great wealth, would have provided sanctuary for men of scholarship as well as the faithful. Life was harsh and brutal and in 1170 Britain's most famous martyr, Thomas à Becket, Archbishop of Canterbury, was murdered in his Cathedral by an angry King to whom he refused his obedience.

It was a time of great pilgrimages and one such pilgrimage has been immortalised in Chaucer's *Canterbury Tales*. On that occasion the shrine was Canterbury and the saint was the murdered archbishop Thomas à Becket. But the tragic era of the Crusades (1096–1291), with its aim of the capture of the Holy Land from the infidels, was to sap much of the wealth and enterprise of the whole of Christian Europe. Richard I of England (Cœur de Lion), much loved and admired by his people, typified the ideals of his times even though the crusade he led failed to capture Jerusalem. Perhaps despite the savagery of those times they will be remembered for the marvellous creativity of their builders and for the great ideals that inspired peasants and kings to embark upon incredibly dangerous holy wars to foreign lands.

Every country has its time of greatness and for England it is the Elizabethan Age, which for sheer exuberance, inventiveness and boldness has never been surpassed. Our language was enriched by some of the greatest literature ever written, and although the name of Shakespeare stands supreme, poetry and music was produced in great profusion. The fact that English is probably the most important language in the world is a testimony to these Elizabethan pioneers and explorers who, as a tiny nation of some three million people living on a small island in the North Sea, ventured so far and achieved so much.

Scotland ever since Roman times has remained proudly independent and its fierce tribesmen, aided by an inhospitable and mountainous terrain, made occupation extremely difficult. The Scots under Robert the Bruce repulsed the English armies under Edward I at their most celebrated victory of Bannockburn in 1314. Under the great religious leader John Knox, Calvinism was established as the national religion and the fierce puritanism of his teachings are still reflected in the character of the Scottish people. But inevitably union with the more powerful England had to come, although this did not take place until 1707. The Jacobite risings led by the darling of Scottish romance, Bonnie Prince Charlie, were a tragic failure and the punitive manner in which the Highlanders were pursued and punished is a bitter memory to many Scots even to this day. The discovery of important oilfields in the North Sea has coincided with an upsurge in Scottish nationalism and reveals a deep division in Scottish opinion as to her relationship with England. Perhaps it reflects a world-wide paradox in which the interests of small communities and groups of all kinds seem more and more to be threatened by take-overs at a time when there is an unparalleled rise in the expectations and hopes of individual human beings.

The other important nation that goes to make up Britain is Wales. Unlike Scotland, large numbers of Welsh people speak their own native language, although sadly in recent years English is slowly replacing it. Wales was incorporated into England politically in 1536 during the reign of Henry VIII and until that time it had stoutly defended its independence against the Saxons and later the Norman invaders. Coal-mining, which has flourished since the eighteenth century, is now an important part of Welsh folk-lore. Mining disasters and pit closures have brought much tragedy into Welsh homes and this is reflected in their songs and the character of their literature. Non-conformism has also been a powerful factor in Welsh life, and the Welsh are an articulate as well as musical people. The countryside of Wales is, like Scotland, mountainous and rugged, and sheep farming has for a long time been the staple occupation of Welsh farmers. As with the Scots there are powerful elements in Wales who desire independence from England although most Welsh people are now recognising that such a move would be economically risky.

The one-time British Empire 'Upon whose flag the sun never set' reached the peak of its pomp and splendour under Queen Victoria. During her reign Britain developed fast, experiencing a population explosion as well as a sudden surge forward in all forms of engineering. Home-produced coal and the steam engine were the tools which made Britain in her time the world's first industrial power. Britain ruled the seas with the largest navy the world had ever seen. Its small but professional army occupied strategic bases all over the world. British missionaries penetrated into the remotest areas and everywhere 'trade followed the flag'. The First World War with its unprecedented losses in men and the consequent deterioration in morale brought Britain a Pyrrhic victory. The between-war period was characterised by unemployment, poverty and bitterness. The Second World War, during which Britain inspired the free world by her lone stand against a vastly superior enemy, brought much destruction to her cities. Victory was achieved at a great cost and the aftermath of the war brought enormous changes. The nations that made up the British Empire, beginning with India, opted for self-government and independence and in the climate of the post-war world Britain did nothing to discourage or oppose these natural aspirations. The result is that a great Commonwealth of Nations, many of whom still recognise the Queen as their non-political head, has evolved. Although many of the ties are very nebulous, the annual meeting of the Commonwealth is an event which is taken seriously and much goodwill comes from these world-wide get-togethers.

The latest landmark in British history has undoubtedly been its membership of the European Community. The British people in a referendum gave positive support for this momentous new venture which for so many years they had resisted. The great ideals of this community of nations have yet to be realised. If Europe does succeed in creating this new continental state in which peoples of vastly different ways of life trade and co-exist successfully then this little North Sea Island of Britain which has contributed so much to the world will no doubt continue to play an important part. But come what may Britain has written its name large in the pages of the world's history book and perhaps it could borrow the words of the famous French song and say simply: 'Je ne regrette rien'.

ENGLAND

It has never been difficult for a writer to wax lyrical about England, its countryside and its rich heritage. Few people, from England or abroad, fail to carry an instant impression of the country in their mind's eye. Just as the mention of Christmas evokes the instant response in the imagination of food, snow, warmth and jollity, so the mind's eye carries equally vivid, sometimes contradictory, images of England. Again, they will probably be sentimental and old-fashioned (though who can imagine Christmas without television now, and how many snug, thatched cottages are without aerials sprouting from their chimneys?). Yet there is much more to our countryside than the standard scenes too often displayed on calendars and chocolate boxes. Most seasoned travellers know that the only way to discover the true flavour of a country is to explore the places furthest from the track beaten by the majority of tourists. The trouble is that in England there are so many different flavours. Traditionally, the village inn is the best place to discover regional characteristics, but since it is the delight of the Englishman to be an individual, the inns in neighbouring villages will each offer such diversity of opinions, such differing versions of history, that professional travellers who elect to 'discover' the country by this method are left bemused. This is reflected in the bizarre picture of England presented in their writings, and so the myth goes on.

Thus the methods of exploration should be subtle. A stranger can appear gullible to encourage the born storyteller, but can accept the information with the proverbial pinch of salt. So it is with the routes that he chooses to travel. There are places that are made to seem obligatory to every visitor to England, and this is not to decry them (especially Westminster Abbey, shown *opposite*), but if he restricts himself to the popular excursions he misses out on many of the best treasures of England which successfully hide themselves from the eyes of all except those with the determination to track them down or those who stumble across them by accident. This brief introduction is thus a concentration of places which, though not neccesarily illustrated in the following pages, are well worth discovering. They are off the main routes, and just getting to them is adventure itself.

Firstly look for Wycoller in eastern Lancashire, near the cotton towns of Colne and Nelson, and not far from Haworth (which is the picturesque centre of the Brontë industry). Wycoller is reached by a twisting country lane, which eventually leads to a straggle of old cottages, a packhouse bridge over a moorland stream, and the remains of Wycoller Hall. This late-sixteenth-century building is said to have inspired 'Ferndean Manor' in *Jane Eyre*.

Then there is Holkham on the coast of north Norfolk. The great Palladian hall, the seat of the Earls of Leicester, is one of the grandest of country houses and is well worth visiting, but equally deserving is the wild stretch of coastline here. This often seems to be the nearest thing to a desert island that England can offer.

For countless years Rutland was a joke to the English. With a breadth of little more than twelve miles its aspirations as a county seemed hilarious, yet until the mid-1970s it retained its independence. Since then the counties of England have been shuffled and local government 'rationalised', and in theory Rutland vanished into the bottomless horror of bureaucracy. Despite this, and the fact that its loveliest valleys have been lost beneath the waters of a reservoir, Rutland's landscape survives. Its gentle countryside still retains hedges, that essentially English feature that is vanishing in the richer farming counties, and its small villages and country towns present an unspoilt picture of rural life.

The country towns of England are one of the priceless treasures of our English heritage. Here the visitor will find cameos that reflect the best of our architectural history as well as its present character. An after-dinner wander through a town such as Oakham, Marlborough, Totnes, or Beverley will reveal individual buildings with even more character than the famous places that owe their popularity to the extravagance of their Tudor or Georgian architecture. The humble parish church often reflects the nuances of history far more graphically than the grand cathedral, and if one is fortunate enough to visit a country town on market day, with auctions of produce and 'cottage furniture' in full swing, then the splendid pageantry of modern country life will be discovered – complete with its medieval overtones!

It would be easy to continue in this vein from shore to shore, town to town, even street to street. Still unmentioned are the beautiful byways of Cornwall – the lonely cliff-top paths that look down on tiny rock-strewn inlets that were once the haunt of wreckers and smugglers. Or there is the other side of Cornwall – the lovely estuarine villages of the south, like Helford or St Anthony, with cottages hidden among lush vegetation. To the east there is the wonderful coastline of the Isle of Purbeck, immortalised by Thomas Hardy, wide areas of which are still unfrequented. Or there are the lonely acres of Breckland in Norfolk and Suffolk, much of it covered in forest, which has a special magic on a hot summer's day when the rich scent of resin fills the air and the numerous herds of deer move lazily from clearing to clearing. Such scenes are just a hint of the elements that make a memory of England so enduring, its heritage a unique blend of the works of man and of Nature.

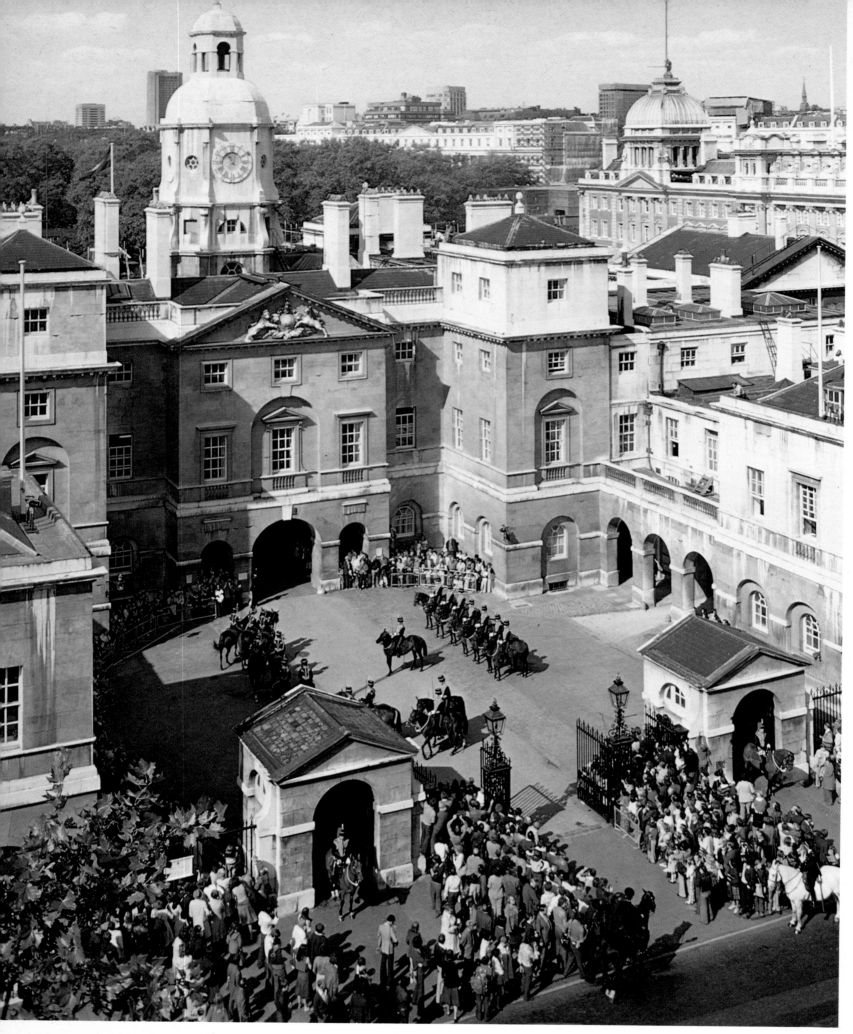

The English are famed throughout the world for their spectacular and precisely ordered traditional ceremonies, and the pomp and pageantry of London forms one of the most exciting aspects of this great capital city. Mounting the Guard (*above*) takes place every morning when the guard is changed at Horse Guards, a square situated just to the west of Whitehall. Probably the most impressive London ceremony is of Trooping the Colour which is held annually on the Queen's official birthday.

Escape from the noise and bustle of the city for a few minutes in Trafalgar Square, where fountains play and the strutting pigeons are so tame that they will feed trustingly from your hand (*above*). Trafalgar Square was laid out between 1829 and 1841 in honour of Admiral Lord Nelson's great naval victory. The focal point of the Square is Nelson's Column, almost 185 feet high, with Landseer's four bronze lions at its base. To the north-east is the beautiful church of St Martin-in-the-Fields, built in the Classical style by James Gibbs in 1726.

London is rich in landmarks, the most prominent being St Paul's Cathedral (*above*), situated on the crown of Ludgate Hill in the historic square mile of the City. St Paul's is the largest church in England and was built by Sir Christopher Wren after the Great Fire of 1666 destroyed a Norman church which had stood on this site. Equally impressive architecturally are the Houses of Parliament (*above right*), overlooking the River Thames. Parliament was built on the site of the ancient Palace of Westminster, most of which was destroyed by fire in 1834. This is probably the largest Gothic building in the world and contains over 500 apartments as well as the House of Lords, the House of Commons and the Clock Tower. Although the Clock Tower is commonly known as Big Ben, this title really only applies to the immense hour bell. Tower Bridge (*right*) is a masterpiece of design and precision engineering. Its great bascules can be raised in a matter of minutes to allow ships to pass underneath, and its mechanism has never failed since the bridge was opened in 1894.

Despite its proximity to London, the county of Kent is aptly known as the 'Garden of England' and orchards have
flourished here from Roman times to the present day because of its fertile soil, regular rainfall and mild climate. The fertility
of the soil is due to its high iron content, and Kent was also once a centre for iron-founding, although this industry vanished
several centuries ago. The last forge to close down, in 1765, was situated at Lamberhurst. Today this small village on the
London to Hastings road has kept much of its ancient character, and has several half-timbered houses. About a mile away
is the ruined Scotney Old Castle (*above*) which consists of the remains of a round tower, dating from 1377, and parts of a
Tudor mansion. These romantic relics, surrounded by a moat, are set in beautifully landscaped gardens. The castle is
supposedly haunted by an eighteenth-century revenue man who was murdered in cold blood and his body thrown into the
moat.

Surrey, while not quite so fruitful as the neighbouring Kent, is still a green and pleasant county with a great abundance of trees and garden lands contrasting with open commons. The scenery here is indeed very varied and includes the chalk ridge of the North Downs which crosses the county from east to west and finally narrows into the scenic Hog's Back. Also in the county is Leith Hill, which at 965 feet is the highest point in south-east England. Surrey is sometimes called 'the Cockneys' Back Yard' and it is a popular dormitory area for London, so that its north-eastern parts nearest to the capital have become built-up. The major part of the county remains more or less unspoilt, however, and there are many delightful towns and villages to visit. Guildford, for instance, in the valley of the River Wey, has a remarkable mixture of old and new architecture, ranging from the ruins of a Norman castle to the modern cathedral. From Guildford a road runs along the Hog's Back to Farnham, one of the best preserved towns in the district. Many of the houses here are Georgian but there are also some fine examples of half-timbered Tudor buildings, and Farnham is dominated by its twelfth-century castle. The smaller Surrey villages are no less interesting; Shere (*below*) is a beautiful village nestling under the North Downs by the banks of the River Tillingbourne. The church here is Norman. One mile to the west is the Silent Pool, in which a Saxon maiden was tragically drowned and is now supposed to haunt the spot. One of the greatest lakes in this area is Virginia Water, right on the Surrey border. This artificial lake was created during the reign of George III from dammed-up streams. On its southern shore stands a group of ancient pillars brought from Lepis Magna in Tripoli by order of George IV, and nearby is an observatory, which had to be rebuilt after the original building was burnt to the ground in the eighteenth century.

The most important geographical feature of Sussex is the chalk scarp of the South Downs which runs parallel to the coastline and forms the backbone of the county. Sussex is actually divided into two counties, East and West, each with a distinctive character. West Sussex has lush, well-wooded scenery and steep hills. Chichester is the most important town, while on the coast are such popular seaside resorts as Bognor Regis, Worthing and Littlehampton. East Sussex has a more gentle and open aspect, offering wonderful panoramas across the South Downs. It is rich in ancient and historical buildings too, and one of the most romantic is Bodiam Castle (*left*). This dates from the fourteenth century and was the last military castle to be built in England – it was erected as a defence against French invasion. Although its main role was that of a fortress, it was also one of the first castles to be designed as a comfortable residence. Bodiam Castle is beautifully situated in the centre of a large moat scattered with water-lilies, and although it is now roofless, it has been remarkably well preserved. The East Sussex coastline (once a haunt of smugglers) has a string of popular resorts, backed by splendid cliffs, and the largest of these holiday towns is Brighton. Once Brighton was just a small fishing village but in 1754 it was made fashionable by Dr Russell, who advocated sea-bathing as a cure for most ills. Since then, Brighton has prospered, and its crowning glory is the Chinese-style Pavilion built by the Prince Regent (later King George IV), who often brought his court here. A little further along the coast is Eastbourne, another favourite holiday town, and Hastings (*below*). Hastings is most notable as the base from which William the Conqueror set out to fight the Battle of Hastings some six miles away. Hastings later became a Cinque Port and a fishing centre, thriving until its once excellent harbour silted up. Today Hastings has become a holiday centre but fishing is still carried on in the area known as the Old Town. However, since there is no longer a harbour, the boats have to be hauled up on to the shingle beaches. The town and beaches are overlooked by the ruins of Hastings Castle, and nearby are St Clement's Caves, a fascinating network of sandstone caves which extend for about three acres.

The Royal County of Berkshire (it was granted this title in 1957) lies entirely within the basin formed by the River Thames. Parts of Berkshire have become London dormitory areas but to the south-west are the flat meadows in the valley of the River Kennet, and beyond are rolling chalk downlands. Here is Inkpen Hill which, at a height of almost 1,000 feet, is the highest chalk down in England. On its summit is the gruesome Combe Gibbet. The county town of Berkshire is Reading, but the most historic town is Windsor, situated on the bank of the River Thames and dominated by its great castle. Windsor Castle is the largest inhabited castle in the world, covering almost thirteen acres, and it has been used as a royal residence for more than 850 years. A fortress was first founded here by William the Conqueror in the eleventh century, although none of this original castle survives. The existing building was begun, in stone, by Henry II and successive monarchs made additions and alterations right up until the reign of Queen Victoria. The castle is made up of three parts: the Lower, Middle and Upper Wards. The Lower Ward contains St George's Chapel, founded by Edward III, which ranks as England's finest example of Perpendicular architecture. The Chapel is now the burial place for royalty, and is also the official church of the Knights of the Garter, an order which was founded by Edward III in 1348. Every year the Knights of the Order of the Garter walk in procession (*above*) to St George's Chapel for their formal installation. The Middle Ward incorporates Henry II's massive Round Tower, while in the Upper Ward are the State Apartments and the Sovereign's private apartments. The State Apartments house a priceless collection of paintings, furniture, porcelain and armour. Around the Castle is the Home Park, which extends for about 400 acres, and the Great Park which incorporates some 4,800 acres of wooded parkland and magnificent gardens, including the Savill Garden, the Valley Garden and the Japanese Kurune Punch Bowl, all ablaze with rhododendrons and innumerable other plants. A bridge across the Thames separates Windsor from Eton. Eton has a charming old High Street which leads to Eton College, the famous Public School founded in 1440 by King Henry VI.

Hampshire is always associated with the New Forest, a great tract of countryside covering an area of 144 square miles. The New Forest was established in 1079 by William the Conqueror, who ordered the afforestation of this area so that it would provide him with a good hunting ground. Today it has one of the greatest varieties of trees in England, with beeches, oaks and birches as the predominating species, but it is not completely wooded as there are also thousands of acres of open heath and, of course, the gardens and cultivated lands of the inhabitants of the Forest. Deer live in the Forest, and wild donkeys, but the most unique attraction must be the New Forest ponies who graze here. It is usually presumed that these hardy little ponies are wild, but in fact this is not the case as they are all privately owned now, although they may be descended from the truly wild horses that lived here in Norman times. The Forest, of course, is rich in history, and twenty-two Saxon villages are supposed to lie beneath the ground here. More evident is the Rufus Stone, near Minstead, which marks the spot where William II was killed by an arrow in 1100. The 'capital' of the New Forest is Lyndhurst but all the villages seem to be equally attractive with their wide streets, village greens and thatched cottages such as these at Swan Green (*below*). The New Forest is only one element of Hampshire, however. Much of the rest of the county consists of rolling chalk uplands, or sandy tracts carpeted with gorse and heather, and with all these open spaces it is hardly surprising that Hampshire should have been the birthplace of that peculiarly English game, cricket. The first cricket club was set up at Hambledon in 1760. Hampshire's county town is Winchester which, with its magnificent Norman cathedral, is also a great religious centre. A totally different face of Hampshire is provided by its coastline. Here are many flourishing holiday resorts, such as Lymington, and here also are the great ports of Southampton and Portsmouth. Southampton is commercially important as well as a seaport, and it is Britain's busiest port for ships. Because of its position opposite the Isle of Wight it is favoured with four high tides a day. In 1620 the Pilgrim Fathers sailed out from here aboard the *Mayflower* at the start of their historic voyage to America. Portsmouth was England's chief naval base for many centuries and its first dock was built as long ago as 1194 by Richard I, and then the first dry dock in the world was erected here in 1495. The dockyards were further developed from the seventeenth century onwards, and today Portsmouth is still an important naval port and submarines can often be seen here amongst the more usual shipping. Carefully preserved in the dockyard is Nelson's flagship *Victory*, which saw action at the Battle of Trafalgar.

Wiltshire is one of the more lonely and spacious English counties, where towns and villages tend to be scattered far apart, and because of this relative inaccessibility it has escaped the ravages of urban development. The county town is Salisbury, a historic place that was founded, along with its cathedral, in the thirteenth century. Salisbury Cathedral is a perfect example of Early English church architecture and its spire, 404 feet high, is the tallest in England. Of Wiltshire's many villages, Castle Combe (*left*) is probably the most attractive, and indeed it has been voted the 'Prettiest Village in England'. It is set in a deep wooded valley on the banks of a placid stream and the cottages, which are built from mellow stone, cluster around an old market cross. In medieval times Wiltshire was a prosperous centre of weaving and Castle Combe was once a weaving town; the Weaver's House (to which cloth was taken after it had been woven) can still be seen. The Wiltshire landscape is made up of valleys, low-lying agricultural land, forests, water-meadows and great expanses of downland such as the Marlborough Downs and Salisbury Plain. Few areas in England are more steeped in history. Running along the rest of the Marlborough Downs is the prehistoric track known as the Ridgeway, surrounded by the remains of several hill forts. In the heart of these Downs is Avebury stone circle, one of the largest prehistoric monuments in Europe. An earthwork, thought to be 4,000 years old, encloses the remains of the stone circle, which dates from the Bronze Age. When first built, it consisted of about 100 standing stones with two smaller circles within. In the vicinity are many more earthworks, circles and barrows as well as the mysterious Silbury Hill, an enormous prehistoric man-made mound. The purpose for which this was built remains unexplained. Wiltshire's greatest prehistoric relic, however, is Stonehenge (*below*), an incredible circle of standing stones rising above the bleak chalk landscape of Salisbury Plain. At first Stonehenge consisted of only a bank and a ditch, but during the Neolithic era about eighty massive blue stones were somehow transported here from Wales, and arranged in two concentric circles. The monument was completed in the Bronze Age, when an outer circle of lintelled uprights and an inner circle of trilithons were erected. The blue stones were later replaced within these circles. As with the Avebury stone circle, the true function of Stonehenge has never been determined. Probably it had some sort of religious significance but almost certainly it was used to calculate the annual calendar and the seasons, because the axis of Stonehenge was precisely aligned with sunrise on 21 June, the longest day in the year. Sun-worshipping ceremonies are believed to have been held here once, and to this day the Companions of the Most Ancient Order of Druids gather here to watch the sun rise on 21 June.

Dorset is Thomas Hardy country and the scenery which so inspired him remains almost unchanged since he described it in his novels. Hardy was a native of Bockhampton and many of the surrounding towns feature in his books, thinly disguised under different names – for instance Shaftesbury is called by its old name of 'Shaston'. Overlooking the Blackmoor Vale, Shaftesbury is Dorset's oldest hill-top town, and the cobbled Gold Hill (*right*) is terraced with houses clinging precariously to the steep hillside. King Canute died in this town in 1035. Nearby is Moreton, where T. E. Lawrence (better known as Lawrence of Arabia) lies buried in the churchyard. He was killed in a motor-cycle crash in 1935. For such a comparatively small county, the scenery of Dorset is remarkably varied. Inland, wild stretches of lonely heath and marshlands vie with wooded copses and undulating agricultural country. Blandford Forum and its outlying hamlets such as Hilton (*below*) form the hub of the farming community. There are also many traces of a much older Dorset. Maiden Castle, near Dorchester, is one of Europe's largest and best-preserved fortified earthworks, dating from the Iron Age, while at Corfe Castle are the dramatic remains of a Norman castle. King Edward the Martyr was murdered here in AD 978 and in 1646 the Castle was besieged by Cromwell. Equally dramatic is the Cerne Abbas Giant, an enormous figure carved in the turf of the chalk hillside overlooking the village of Cerne Abbas. The coastline of Dorset stretches for about seventy miles and again offers a great diversity of scenery, from pleasant sandy beaches to rugged cliffs with strange rock formations and contorted strata. The most remarkable stratified cliffs are those of Stair Hole at Lulworth Cove, and a mile to the west stands the famous Durdle Door, a headland from which an arch has been cut in the rock by the action of the sea. Another interesting geological feature on this coastline is the Chesil Bank, a sixteen-mile-long reef of shingle extending from Abbotsbury to Portland and enclosing a lagoon known as the Fleet. The bank is composed of pebbles graduated in size, with the smallest at its western end. The arm of Chesil Bank provides shelter for the attractive and popular resort of Weymouth and it also connects the Isle of Portland to the mainland. Portland is a rocky peninsula scarred with stone quarries (St Paul's Cathedral was built from Portland stone) and it is now used as a major naval harbour. Dorset's most important harbour, however, is at Poole, which is also the county's largest town. Its harbour is natural and is almost land-locked with a shoreline measuring nearly 100 miles. Once Poole harbour was used by pirates as a base from which to rob Spanish and French galleons, and its mass of creeks and inlets were also favoured by smugglers. Today it is always crowded with colourful yachts and is also often used as a base for the increasingly popular sport of shark fishing. On the quay itself, visitors can watch pottery being made.

Devon is particularly fortunate in having two coasts. The northern coast is the most impressive with its chain of louring cliffs dipping straight to the sea, and the wide expanse of Bideford Bay. Two of the most charming but also the most spectacular villages here are Lynton and Lynmouth. Lynton is perched high on a cliff-top and, almost vertically beneath it, by the sea, is Lynmouth (*right*). The two are connected by a cliff railway. Disaster struck Lynmouth in 1952 when its river flooded after a freak storm and swept away almost one hundred houses. Just to the west is the eerie Valley of the Rocks, where jutting pinnacles rear their heads some 800 feet above the sea. The greatest natural feature of Devon, however, is Dartmoor, a massive upland expanse of granite which occupies a considerable portion of South Devon. Once a royal hunting ground, Dartmoor was made a National Park in 1951. Its best known features are the tors; great knobs of granite which protrude from the peat-covered ground. Yes Tor, at 2,028 feet, is one of the highest of these tors. The moor is in parts an isolated and utterly bleak place, particularly around the grim prison at Princetown, and in these surroundings it is easy to believe in the legends of pixies, ghosts and demons which have been passed down over the centuries. The northern moors are rich in prehistoric relics such as the hut circle at Grimspound, but the scenery to the south is more gentle, with tiny villages, meandering streams, woodland, waterfalls, and open ground where the famous Dartmoor ponies can graze. Dartmeet, where two rivers converge, is one of the most famous beauty spots on the moor. Devon's southern coastline boasts some of the finest resorts in the west of England, including Torquay, Teignmouth, Sidmouth and the great port of Dartmouth, which is dominated by the Royal Naval College. Brixham (*below*) was once the most important fishing port in Devon, with a fleet of 300 trawlers, and this industry still thrives. It was here, in 1688, that William of Orange first set foot in England.

Cornwall is a long tapering peninsula which culminates at the aptly named Land's End, where the jagged granite cliffs mark the most westerly point of England, once thought to be the end of the world. Like its neighbouring county of Devon, Cornwall also has two coasts, great scenic variety, and a sub-tropical climate. The land is steeped in legend, particularly at Tintagel, which is associated with King Arthur and Merlin. The remains of an ancient castle stand on the cliff-top here and there is also a fine fourteenth-century manor house which has now become the Tintagel Post Office (*above*). The whole county has a Continental flavour and, indeed, is often known as the 'Cornish Riviera', for the mild climate allows exotic plants such as palm trees to grow, while the villages have brightly painted cottages which are often arranged in tiers. Numerous fishing hamlets are scattered around the coast, and one such is the beautiful Mullion Cove (*right*), once a smugglers' haunt. Just beyond Mullion is Poldhu Point from where, in 1901, the first transatlantic morse signals were transmitted.

Somerset is often referred to as the 'Gateway to the West'. Farming is a major industry in this fertile county, as is implied by its Old English name which means 'the land of the summer-farm dwellers'. Its natural landscape is that of a plain surrounded by hills; to the north-east is the limestone range of the Mendips, in the south are the Blackdown Hills, while to the north-west are the undulating Quantock Hills and the heather-clad Exmoor National Park, whose boundaries reach over into Devon. Exmoor was the setting for *Lorna Doone*, the romantic novel by R. D. Blackmore. One of the most interesting features of the county is the fine church architecture. Of all the many Somerset churches, the greatest is Wells Cathedral (*left*), which possesses the most complete group of ecclesiastical buildings in England. The cathedral was begun in 1180, but it incorporates many later stages of architecture, such as the Early English west front decorated with magnificent sculptures. At Glastonbury, one of the most holy spots in Britain, are the remains of an ancient abbey. Glastonbury is sometimes associated with Avalon, that legendary place from the tales of King Arthur, and legend also relates that Joseph of Arimathea buried the Holy Grail (the chalice used at the Last Supper) beneath the Chalice Spring on Glastonbury Tor.

Avon is one of the smallest counties in England yet it contains two historic cities, Bristol and Bath, within its boundaries. Because of its situation on the River Avon, Bristol has been for centuries a busy port and a centre for trade and commerce. Bath owes its fame to its warm mineral springs, around which the Romans built a complex of baths. By the eighteenth century, Bath had developed into the most fashionable spa in the country and, under the influence of the dandy Beau Nash, became a meeting place for High Society. It was at this time that the elegant terraces, parks and crescents, such as Lansdown Crescent (*above*) were built and Bath remains the finest example of a Georgian city in Britain.

Gloucestershire possesses three distinct landscapes: the pastoral Severn Vale, the enchanting woodlands of the Forest of Dean (beneath which lies a vast coalfield) and the fifty-mile-long range of the Cotswold Hills. The Cotswolds, with their pellucid trout streams and close-cropped meadows divided by dry stone walls, have been sheep-country for many centuries, although it was the fifteenth century that saw the height of the wool trade here. In many cases, the handsome Cotswold churches were built as a mark of gratitude for their success by rich wool merchants. Chipping Campden (*left*) was the home of some of the wealthiest of the wool merchants in the Middle Ages, and its architecture reflects their prosperity. It has many gabled houses, built in the mellow stone which is such a distinctive feature of Cotswold architecture, as well as a fine church and the lovely Jacobean market hall which has arches and a timber roof. Two of the prettiest little villages in the district are Upper Slaughter (*above*) and Lower Slaughter, both of which have a stream running through them. The city and inland port of Gloucester, which gave the country its name, was founded as a Roman fort at the lowest crossing of the River Severn, to guard the route into Wales. The Normans walled the city, built a castle (later destroyed) and founded the imposing Gloucester Cathedral which still retains its basic Norman structure, but also has many additions from later architectural periods. For centuries, the city has been an inland port, with mile upon mile of waterways, and about three miles down-river from Gloucester, the strange natural phenomenon known as the Severn Bore sometimes occurs at certain high tides. This is a small tidal wave which can reverse the flow of the river and can attain a height of six feet and a speed of thirteen miles per hour.

Oxfordshire lies in the basin of the River Thames and stretches out into a great plain towards the crest of the Cotswolds in the west and the chalk scarp of the Chiltern Hills in the east. The city of Oxford, 'that sweet city with her dreaming spires', has the second oldest university in Europe, founded in the thirteenth century. The earliest colleges were University, Balliol and Merton, but the largest is Christ Church. Among the many other notable buildings in the city are the Radcliffe Camera, the Bodleian Library and the Ashmolean Museum. A little to the north of Oxford is another architectural masterpiece, Blenheim Palace (*above left*), which was designed by Sir John Vanbrugh. This vast mansion was built in 1705 for the Duke of Marlborough, one of England's greatest soldiers, as a reward for his victory against the French at Blenheim in 1704. The surrounding parkland was laid out by Capability Brown.

Northamptonshire is often called 'the county of spires and squires' because its rolling landscape is so often punctuated by churches and great country houses. A prime example is Kirby Hall (*left*), near the village of Gretton, which is now classed as an Ancient Monument. This splendid Elizabethan mansion was begun in 1570 and was modernised in the seventeenth century by Inigo Jones. Although the house appears intact from the exterior, only a few rooms are still complete, as the rest fell into ruin in the last century. There is a huge inner courtyard and some particularly fine rose gardens. Some few miles away is the historic village of Fotheringhay; historic yet tragic, for in the now-ruined castle here Mary Queen of Scots was beheaded in 1587.

From Oxfordshire, the great Chiltern Hills stretch into the county of Buckinghamshire. In prehistoric times a vast forest covered the Chilterns and part of this survives today at Burnham Beeches (*above*), a glorious 600-acre expanse of beech trees and mossy glades which are carpeted with bluebells in the spring. The Buckinghamshire villages are delightful and many of them have associations with famous people. Jordans is the burial place of William Penn, the Quaker who founded Pennsylvania, and there is a simple Friends' Meeting House here, containing many relics of the first Quakers. Hughenden, near High Wycombe, was once the home and is now the final resting place of the great statesman Benjamin Disraeli, while the philosopher Edmund Burke is buried at Beaconsfield. Famous for quite different reasons was Sir Francis Dashwood, who founded the notorious 'Hell Fire Club' which held its meetings at Medmenham and West Wycombe. Literary figures are well represented too, especially by Milton, who finished *Paradise Lost* and wrote *Paradise Regained* at his cottage in Chalfont St Giles, and Mary Shelley, who worked on *Frankenstein* when she lived at Marlow with her husband, the poet Percy Bysshe Shelley.

Warwickshire is inextricably linked with one of the greatest writers the world has ever known, William Shakespeare, who often used the surrounding countryside as the setting for his plays. The Forest of Arden, for instance, which features in *As You Like It*, once covered much of north Warwickshire. Shakespeare was born in 1564 in the old market town of Stratford-upon-Avon, at a house in Henley Street. Among other buildings in Stratford that are directly associated with the Bard are his son-in-law's house, Hall's Croft; the remains of his own home, New Place; the Guildhall, where he was educated; and Holy Trinity Church (*left*), in which he is buried. His tomb is marked by a simple engraved stone. Shakespeare is best commemorated, however, by the Royal Shakespeare Theatre where a festival of his plays is held every year. A mile away from Stratford is the village of Shottery, where Shakespeare's wife, Anne Hathaway, once lived. Anne Hathaway's Cottage is a typical English country cottage (albeit a rather large cottage as it has twelve rooms) with a thatched roof and charming gardens. The Town Crier is pictured here (*above*) outside the cottage. In contrast, the county's most impressive building is the thirteenth-century Warwick Castle, which stands on a dramatic cliff overlooking the River Avon. The State Apartments (*overleaf*) house a magnificent collection of armour and paintings.

Staffordshire and the West Midlands are often known collectively as the Black Country, for they are areas of great industrial activity connected with coal mines, steelworks and potteries. Yet even in the manufacturing centres here there are many things of beauty to be found, such as the half-timbered Oak House (*above*) in West Bromwich. The Midland area of England is altogether often grossly underrated, for the industrial areas make up just a small part of the scenery. Throughout the Midlands there are many unspoilt villages like Upton Snodsbury (*below*) in Hereford and Worcester, as well as mile upon mile of unspoilt countryside. Symond's Yat (*right*) is a noted beauty spot, where the River Wye flows through a narrow gorge in a great loop, almost doubling back upon itself.

Ludlow is the most historic town in Shropshire, with its massive castle built in 1085. In 1634 *Comus*, a masque by John Milton, was first performed at this castle. Other ancient buildings in Ludlow include the half-timbered Feathers Hotel, and the 300-year-old Angel Inn where Lord Nelson once stayed. The Morris Dancers pictured here (*left*) outside the inn bring a touch of tradition to a long, peaceful summer's afternoon. The origins of Morris dancing are now lost in the mists of history, but the Morris Men are usually acting out old legends in their ritual dances. The dancers are decorated with ribbons, flowers and bells and traditionally they used to be accompanied by other characters (the Fool, for instance) who did not actually take part in the dance. The pace of life in Britain is often slow and tranquil, reflected by peaceful villages such as Burbage (*above*) in Leicestershire.

Much of England is lush pastureland, and some of the richest grazing land can be found in Leicestershire. Lying in the basin of the River Soar, this county has some marvellous waterside scenery, while it is also criss-crossed by a network of canals. Even the reservoirs here attract a wide variety of wildfowl; one of the most frequented reservoirs is situated at the bottom of a steep hillside, overlooked by the village of Stoke Dry. Here at Stoke Dry is a fine country church, dedicated to St Andrew, so typical of the simple yet dignified church architecture which is frequently found in the English countryside. The interior of St Andrew's (*right*) is plain and quite unelaborate yet it provides a complete and meaningful record of local history, commemorated by such features as carvings, windows and, above all, tombs. The most notable tombs in this church belong to members of the Digby family. Sir Kenelm Digby, who is buried here in a splendid alabaster tomb, was a great naval commander, diplomat and author. He also discovered the importance of oxygen to plants. His father, Sir Everard Digby, however, had been executed in 1606 for his part in the Gunpowder Plot of 1605, led by Guy Fawkes, which had aimed to blow up the Houses of Parliament and then stage a Catholic rising in the Midlands.

We now move east across the country into the low-lying fenland districts. All around this part of England are many surviving examples of sturdy box-framed and half-timbered houses, and this illustration (*below*) shows one of the half-timbered buildings at the village of Hemingford Abbots. There are some equally fine buildings in the adjoining village of Hemingford Grey, on the banks of the River Ouse, including a red brick house of 1697, and an eighteenth-century house built from yellow brick. Most important is a manor house which dates from the twelfth century and is, in fact, one of the oldest inhabited houses in England.

Nottinghamshire has a certain amount of industry because of its coalfield belt (immortalised in D. H. Lawrence's powerful novels), and the town of Nottingham, often called the 'Queen of the Midlands', has a long history as a trading centre. Southwell Minster (*left*) is the most majestic building in Nottinghamshire. However, this county is most often associated with the legendary outlaw Robin Hood and his band of Merry Men, who waylaid rich victims in Sherwood Forest and gave the proceeds to the poor. The legend is really based on fact, for Robin Hood actually existed and was probably an outlawed nobleman. His friend and follower, Little John, is buried in Hathersage Churchyard, Derbyshire (*below*).

Derbyshire is noted for its 'adventure country' of the Peak District in the north with its landscape of crags, bleak moors and caves and pot-holes, but it also has the much softer scenery of the Dales in mid-Derbyshire which are traversed by rivers such as the Wye, Dove and Derwent (*above*), shown here near Yorkshire Bridge.

The great plain of Cheshire, surrounded by the heights of North Wales and the Pennines, is an area of rich farmland and rolling countryside watered by the River Dee. Rising above are wooded ridges which were once the site of ancient British fortifications. Cheshire is noted for a distinctive form of architecture, for many of its houses are 'magpie'; box-framed buildings dating from the sixteenth century with darkened timbers contrasting with white plaster. Little Moreton Hall (*above*), near Congleton, is probably the finest specimen of a 'magpie' house in England. This great manor house was built between 1559 and 1580: it stands on three sides of a quadrangle (with the fourth side open to provide a vista of the gardens), and is surrounded by a moat straddled by a stone bridge. The gatehouse leads into a cobbled courtyard. A watch-tower used to stand at the bottom of the gardens but now all that remains of this is a mound. One of the Hall's most impressive rooms is the aptly named Long Gallery, sixty-eight feet in length, which boasts some original panelling, a beamed roof and enormous fire-places decorated with the arms of England and France. Another room has a secret passage, while yet another room is secreted underneath the moat. Many of the rooms, especially the kitchen, contain pieces of their original furniture. The leaded windows which, according to an inscription on one of the beams, were built in 1559 by 'Richard Dale, Carpeder', are particularly fine but the greatest glory of the Hall, however, is its exterior, which is a mass of carved gables and intricate patterns of timber. The house tilts slightly and has had to be strengthened by some modern supports. Little Moreton Hall is now in the care of the National Trust.

Lancashire, Greater Manchester and Merseyside form a major part of the northern industrial belt and there are three main manufacturing areas. Around Blackburn and Preston in Lancashire's Colne Valley there is a region of cotton-weaving, and Greater Manchester also has a weaving tradition which dates back to the fourteenth century, although it did not assume any real importance until the Industrial Revolution when the invention of new spinning machines and the proximity of coal to drive the steam-powered mills led to a dramatic expansion. The city of Manchester itself is the commercial centre of the cotton textile industry, and is also one of Britain's largest ports, although it is an inland port, connected to the River Mersey by the Manchester Ship Canal. Liverpool, the long-established port of Merseyside, claims to be the greatest Atlantic seaport in Europe. As well as its industrial side, however, Liverpool presents a second, contrasting, face for it is noted for its patronage of the arts. The whole of this industrial region has two identities, for existing side by side with the manufacturing towns are acres of unspoilt countryside. For instance, the Trough of Bowland in Lancashire (*above*) is a dramatic fell crossing which stretches from Sykes to Marshaw. The Trough is hemmed in by the heights of Whins Brow and Top O'Blaze Moss, and is surrounded by some of the loveliest moorland in the country. Once this was a bleak and dangerous pass, winding upwards towards the Trough Stone, and it was often used by raiders during the Civil War, but today it can be easily and safely traversed by car, and offers some magnificent views over the dramatic scenery of the moorlands.

Lancashire is famed most of all for its coastline, where lies that Mecca of holidaymakers, Blackpool. The town began to develop as a resort in the eighteenth century when it was discovered as a holiday centre by the factory workers, who used to come here during their time-off. The peak season here is still during the annual Wakes, when the mills and factories of the industrial North and Midlands are closed, but it also attracts millions of visitors from all over the country. Even in autumn the town is still full of excursionists. The sea front with its excellent sands extends for over seven miles and offers fine bathing and fishing. Blackpool is sometimes known as the 'Coney Island' of England and it is certainly the largest and most popular seaside resort in the country. In order to live up to this reputation, it offers every conceivable form of entertainment, including four theatres, four golf courses, three promenades, gardens, conservatories, a Pleasure Beach with a bathing pool and many entertaining side-shows, tennis courts, boating pools, funfairs and numerous stalls selling the world-famous Blackpool Rock (*below*). This rock is a delicious sweet in the form of a stick, with lettering right through it. Everything in Blackpool is on a vast scale but the most dominant feature is undoubtedly Blackpool Tower, which was modelled on the Eiffel Tower in Paris and stands 520 feet high. It incorporates a ballroom, a menagerie and an aquarium. One of the greatest attractions in Blackpool is the fantastic and elaborate illuminations – every year, from September to October, the tower, promenade and beach are spectacularly lit up.

No greater contrast could be imagined than that between the noisy bustle of Blackpool and the solitude and tranquillity of the adjoining county of Cumbria, surely one of the most delightful in England. The atmosphere of peace is reflected in such lovely country houses as Levens Hall, set in 100 acres of parkland. This Elizabethan mansion, converted from a medieval defensive tower, has some fine panelling and plasterwork ceilings, but its most remarkable feature is undoubtedly the Topiary Garden (*right*), which is probably the finest in England and features shrubs such as box, holly and yew trimmed into ornamental shapes. It was designed in about 1701 by Monsieur Beaumont, who had trained at Versailles and had later remodelled the gardens at Hampton Court Palace for James II. The scenery of Cumbria can be likened to that of Scotland in miniature or even the Swiss Alps, for this county encompasses the Lake District; an aptly named National Park where fifteen lakes nestle beneath massive mountain massifs. The placid lakes and dramatic mountains set each other off to perfection and have for centuries provided inspiration to artists, writers and poets alike. Wordsworth, Coleridge and Southey were so drawn to the landscape that they settled here and have been known ever since as the 'Lake Poets'. Windermere, over ten miles long, is the largest of the lakes, and in fact is the largest lake in England. This is an excellent

centre for marine sportsmen as it caters for such activities as fishing, sailing and water-skiing. It is also the headquarters of the Royal Windermere Yacht Club (founded in 1860) which organises some very impressive races on the lake. Of course, the lakes make up only a small portion of the charm of the Lake District for they are greatly enhanced by the grandeur of the mountain ranges towering above them. The Langdale Pikes, though not of immense height, have a special appeal to rock-climbers, as do the rather more treacherous Borrowdale crags. Certainly Borrowdale, by Derwentwater, has the most romantic and wild appearance of all the Lakeland dales. In this vicinity are some of the highest peaks in the district, including Helvellyn which, at 3,118 feet, is the highest point of a great mountain ridge, and the snow-capped Skiddaw (3,053 feet high) which towers above Derwentwater (*page 52*). At Skiddaw's foot lies the market town of Keswick, one of the busiest and most popular towns in the Lake District. Once a centre for wool-marketing and copper mining, it now prospers not only from its tourist industry but also from its graphite mines. Keswick is one of the most important mountaineering centres in Lakeland, and it has a very experienced mountain-rescue team. The towns and villages of the district provide yet a further aspect of its distinctive charm and many of them have literary associations. Ambleside, for instance, was once known as the intellectual heart of the Lake District, for it was the home of Harriet Martineau and the poet Mathew Arnold, while Emerson, George Eliot and Charlotte Brontë were counted among its many visitors. On the shores of Windermere stands Hawkshead village, which was the scene of Wordsworth's boyhood and schooling, and it must have been here that he first learnt to appreciate the delights of Nature. Nearby is Hilltop Farm, Sawrey, which was the home of Beatrix Potter who created such memorable characters as Peter Rabbit and Jemima Puddleduck. The house where Wordsworth was born can still be seen at Cockermouth, while Dove Cottage, in which he spent his final years, can be visited at Grasmere. He is buried in the churchyard at Grasmere, which is a typical Lakeland village. It is a centre for

those who wish to walk and climb yet it is still unspoilt and local shops such as the Gingerbread Shop (*left*) help to retain its original character. One of the smallest and most charming villages is Watendlath, owned by the National Trust. Hugh Walpole used this hamlet as the setting for his novel *Judith Paris*. A tiny beck flows through Watendlath and further downstream this is spanned by a narrow old packhorse bridge known as Ashness Bridge (*above*). This spot commands what must surely be one of the most breathtaking views in the country, stretching across the calm surface of Derwentwater, scattered with several tree-clad little islands, towards Keswick and the hoary peaks of Skiddaw overlooking the town. The scenery around the bridge is delightful too, for here are many woods and some disused quarries, now overgrown with moss and lichen. Overleaf is a view of Derwentwater.

Almost as stunning as the Ashness Bridge vantage point is the view from Blea Tarn Cottage (*below*), which takes in the slopes of the Langdale Pikes in the distance, here coloured in the mellow golden hues of autumn. The typical form of architecture in the Lake District is plain, totally unpretentious and generally pleasing. In the early days farmers lived in rough and ready huts, but these were superseded by sturdy little cottages such as this example, strong enough to withstand fierce winter storms. These cottages are usually built of local stone, plastered over and whitewashed, and finally roofed with the grey slate hewn from the numerous local quarries. Blea Tarn is situated between Great and Little Langdale and, overshadowed by these peaks, it is one of the most sombre of the lakes and provides a direct contrast to the more pastoral lakes such as Buttermere. In fact, Wordsworth used it as a model for the 'Little lowly vale' of his *Solitary*. Its very name, 'Blea', means 'cold'. Although this scene may sound depressing, in reality it is extremely beautiful. However, it looks as though it would be more at home in the Alps than here, for the icy tones of the water, surrounded by stark pine trees, add a glacial quality to the scene. Even more sombre, however, is Wastwater, which is England's deepest lake (256 feet) as well as its most barren. On the south side the menacing Wasdale Screes veer straight into the lake, while to the north stands a splendid range of mountains. Next to the county of Cumbria lies Northumberland, with the smaller counties of Tyne and Wear, Durham and Cleveland below it. These are largely agricultural areas with some heavy industry, especially in the form of shipbuilding around Tyneside. Boats are important at the Northumberland port of Seahouses too (*right*), but these are fishing boats which still ply their traditional trade, or pleasure boats carrying visitors to the Farne Islands, which are famous as a bird sanctuary and as a breeding place for grey seals.

Blanchland, Northumberland, which lies in the secluded valley of the Derwent, has rightly been described as one of the most perfect villages in England. Built as a model form of village in the eighteenth century by Lord Crewe, it contains everything that one would expect of an ideal village: a little square, charming cottages, a parish church which incorporates part of a twelfth-century abbey, and local shops such as the sweet-shop-cum-post-office (*below*). Blanchland is a little haven of civilisation, for it is surrounded by bleak moorlands. Some of the greatest moors in England must be those of North Yorkshire; a region of rugged grandeur constantly changing its appearance with the varying seasons of the year. Every 12 August, with the start of the grouse-shooting season, the moors are invaded by hunters, but normally their solitude is unbroken. The barren scenery of Stonesdale Moor (*right*) is typical. The solitary moors consist of Jurassic sandstone covered with heathland and a variety of flora, yet also in Yorkshire lie the softly agricultural chalk Wolds, mile upon mile of sheep-grazing countryside and also the popular seaside resorts with all modern amenities, such as Scarborough and Whitby. No part of England contains such important monastic remains as Yorkshire and some of the most impressive remains are of the thirteenth-century Whitby Abbey, which stand gaunt and dramatic on a headland. An earlier abbey on this site was destroyed by the Danes in 867.

Some of the Yorkshire moorland villages are very appealing, despite their stern surroundings. Grassington (*top left*) was once a centre for lead-mining, while Kettlewell (*bottom left*) is pictured here spread out across the open landscape. The ancient walled city of York itself was founded by the Romans and by the Middle Ages it had become the second most important city in England, prospering through its wool trade. It still has many traces of medieval buildings. A reminder of things more modern, however, is the National Railway Museum (*above*) which opened in York in 1975.

Like York, the historic city of Cambridge was also founded by the Romans, but its real importance as a centre of learning did not begin until the thirteenth century. At this time Cambridge University was founded by a group of scholars driven from Oxford (that other great centre of learning) by riots. Peterhouse, the first college at Cambridge, was founded in 1280 and by 1475 the number of colleges had grown to twelve, including among them the noble King's College. This latter was begun in 1441 by Henry VI, who also founded King's College Chapel (*left*), which must rank as one of the most beautiful churches in Europe. The nearby county of Norfolk, although best known for the series of lakes which make up the Norfolk Broads, also has a good stretch of coastline with many attractive resorts and villages such as Cley (*above*), overlooked by its eighteenth-century windmill.

Cambridgeshire and Norfolk are just two of the counties which go to make up part of that region of England known as East Anglia. This has most succinctly been described as 'flat', but there is much to recommend the landscape, which is mostly pastoral and agricultural. Parts of the Suffolk landscape have been immortalised by the great artist John Constable, who was born in East Bergholt in 1776. One of his favourite subjects was Flatford Mill (*above*), which now belongs to the National Trust. The greatest glory of Bedfordshire is Woburn Abbey (*right*), which for centuries has been the home of the Dukes of Bedford. The mansion is open to the public and it contains a wonderful collection of art treasures. The Abbey stands in about 3,000 acres of beautiful parkland which has now been turned into a very successful Safari Park.

WALES

Wales is a land of magic as well as song. The Celts who were driven westwards to this, their last refuge, before a host of different invaders over the centuries, were a mystical, poetry-loving people whose beautiful language perfectly reflected their romantic character. The Welsh guard their Celtic ancestry jealously and go to great lengths to protect and promote their language. Modern bards spend just as much time polishing their offerings for the Eisteddfod as did their predecessors in the Golden Age of Wales, before the Norman Invasion.

Romance dominates the verses of the bards and the same quality is to be seen in much of the landscape of Wales. In the north there are two great areas of high mountains – the ranges of Snowdon and Cader Idris – which never fail to appeal to the romantic side of the spirit, leaving feelings of drama, awe and excitement. Snowdon (*right*) is the major summit of the land. It can be reached by the well-trodden footpath from Llanberis itself (the one from the top of the Pass is equally popular) or by the famous rack-and-pinion railway which is the lazy man's route to the top. Certainly the view is superb (if the right day is chosen) with vistas over Anglesey to the Wicklow mountains across the Irish Sea, but the summit is seldom a lonely place, and the proper way to enjoy a mountain is in solitude. In Wales this is easy to find. Fabulous countryside lies 'off the beaten track'. If mountains are favoured then explore the Carnedd Llywellyn range rather than its more illustrious neighbours. A trek from the Conwy valley over the tops to the sea at Llanfairfechan provides the intrepid walker with as rewarding a highland journey as can be found in Britain. There are countless projects for the less ambitious too. The Forestry Commission diligently mark out routes to viewpoints in the forests by marking trees and rocks with paint. A delightful walk (with a fair ration of steep climbs) through the Betws-y-Coed forest leads to the remote and beautiful Llyn Elsi.

Of course, the mountains of Wales are not confined to the north of the country. There are fine highland areas in the south, notably the Brecon Beacons. However, it is true to say that just as the fame of North Wales stems from its mountain scenery, so the South's reputation comes from its magnificent coastline. The melting of the ice-field that covered much of Britain during the last Ice Age (10,000–25,000 years ago) led to a rise in sea-level that drowned many of the valleys of south-west Wales to form great natural harbours such as Milford Haven. Even earlier changes in sea-level can be seen on the Gower peninsula, at Rhossili, where an ancient line of cliffs stands behind existing cliffs and dunes. Geologically the landscape is of outstanding interest, and the factors that have made the scenery over thousands of centuries have given it both rugged splendour and a peaceful beauty. There are beaches of wide, unblemished sand in the far west of Dyfed that rival any to be found elsewhere in Britain. There are craggy cliffs populated by great colonies of seabirds, and sheltered inlets where fishermen can land their delicious catches of lobsters, crabs and other fish. Behind the coastline the countryside is inviting: narrow lanes wander between villages, deeply set between steep banks where bluebells and primroses grow in the spring. This part of Wales is scenically and culturally most akin to England, particularly to Devon and Cornwall. Yet there are still reminders of its Welshness, like the great castle that guards the river at Pembroke. To the east, along the coastline of the Bristol Channel, industry gradually takes over. Before the Industrial Revolution this might have been one of the loveliest parts of Britain, but then a handful of coal-owners and steel-makers made their fortunes from the quiet valleys, and destroyed their beauty for ever. Cardiff and Swansea grew into great cities stimulated by this industry. Both places were of importance before the Age of Steam, and the capital, Cardiff, had a great castle at its heart, the property of the Marquess of Bute. To the north of Cardiff is Caerphilly Castle, the largest in Britain after Windsor, and one of the chain of castles erected by Edward I to assist him in suppressing the troublesome Welsh. There is a fine viewpoint on the Common overlooking the town. At this distance the development of the valleys looks almost attractive – with industry at arm's length. The ruins of the castle dominate the town and it is obvious why the site was so important strategically. Castle Coch, only five miles or so away, is very different. This stronghold, very much smaller than its illustrious neighbour, was restored by the Marquess of Bute in the nineteenth century as a Romantic's dream of a medieval castle; with pointed turrets brightly painted it looks like the home of an enchanted princess.

The diversity of the Welsh landscape is best appreciated in the countryside of Mid-Wales and the Marches (the lands about the borders of Wales which were under constant pressure in the Middle Ages as the Welsh princes struggled to preserve their independence). There is much to beguile the visitor in these remote villages and country towns. A lovely excursion through Mid-Wales could start from Chirk or Oswestry and proceed by way of the road that winds westwards to Llanarmon DC (a beautifully situated little village that has two excellent hotels facing each other at its centre) and then on to Llanrhaedr-ym-Mochnant. Here there could be a diversion to the wonderful waterfall, Pistyll Rhaedr, described by George Borrow in *Wild Wales*. Then onwards to Lake Vyrnwy and over the mountain pass to Bala, a delightful market town at the heart of Welsh Wales.

Caerphilly Castle, Mid-Glamorgan (*above*), is the most impressive of all Welsh castles and, in fact, is the second largest in Britain. The Romans first built a fort on this site and in 1266 Gilbert de Clare, Lord of Glamorgan, erected a castle here. This was destroyed in 1270 and the existing castle was founded soon after. Caerphilly Castle was built solely for defensive purposes, but Castle Coch (*right*), also in Mid-Glamorgan, is pure fantasy, straight out of a fairy tale. Actually it was a medieval fortress but was rebuilt in 1875 as a residence for the Marquess of Bute, and the resulting red-stone building has turreted towers and even a portcullis and drawbridge. Several more castles can be seen on the Gower Peninsula, the 'Land of the Setting Sun', which has a unique, unspoilt landscape made up of downland, limestone headlands and sandy beaches. The sweeping curve of Three Cliffs Bay (*below*) offers some of the finest scenery in the Peninsula.

The seaport of Kidwelly, Dyfed, grew up at the mouth of the Gwendraeth Fawr river in Norman times. There is a fine cruciform church here which was originally the chapel of a Benedictine monastery. The most important building of the town, however, is Kidwelly Castle (*left*), which stands on higher ground on the bank of the river. A fortress was originally built here by the Normans but it was later rebuilt by Henry I as one of a chain of castles constructed to keep the Welsh under control. It was, however, captured several times by the Welsh. Although the castle is ruined, enough of it remains to give a good impression of its original layout. Partially concentric in its design, the castle has a rectangular Inner Ward (built in the eighteenth century by the Chaworth family) with a drum tower at each angle, as well as an Outer Ward which is a segment of a circle. It is protected by a semicircular moat. One of the castle's most interesting features is its chapel, which dates from about 1300 and is situated on the third storey of one of the towers. Across the river stand the remains of a Benedictine priory, which was founded in 1130 but destroyed at the Dissolution of the Monasteries. However, the priory church, in the Decorated style, is still intact.

Some miles away is the River Teifi and a particularly charming point along its course is Cenarth. This village stands on both sides of the river and is connected by a fine old bridge. It also has picturesque falls (*above*) up which salmon leap, for this is an especially good river for salmon fishing. Cenarth is one of the few places where fishing from coracles is still carried out. The coracle is an ancient form of round boat which can be very easily manoeuvred and can turn sharply, even in a fast-flowing stream, although the inexperienced often find it hard to keep afloat. Sadly, the construction of coracles is now a dying art.

St David's is only a small town on the coast of Dyfed, yet it ranks as a cathedral city. In the sixth century David, the patron saint of Wales, founded a cathedral here at Tyddewi or the 'House of David' as the place was then known. He is said to have made this the centre of Christianity in Wales, and after his death it became a place of pilgrimage and his shrine was visited by William the Conqueror, Henry II and Edward I. The present cathedral (*above*) is the third to stand on this site and it was built in purple-hued sandstone in the twelfth century. The tower collapsed in 1220 and later a large part of the structure was destroyed in an earthquake, so the cathedral was not actually completed until 1522, and it was restored in the nineteenth century. From the outside it looks rather sombre but the interior is a thing of supreme beauty and the intricate roof, made from black Irish oak, is particularly lovely. Further up the Dyfed coast are the harbours of Fishguard and Newquay. Newquay (*below right*) is an enchanting place which has a strong Cornish character with its gaily painted houses lining the hillside above the harbour. Dylan Thomas lived here for some time and a great deal of the town's unhurried, mildly eccentric atmosphere was culled for *Under Milk Wood*. Nearby is the village of Goodwick, which was the scene of the rather farcical last invasion of British soil. This took place in 1797 when a French expeditionary force, consisting mainly of ex-convicts, was forced by adverse winds to land here. The men ignored discipline and pillaged the countryside before they could be forced to lay down their arms. Still further around the coast is the seaside town of Aberystwyth, which lies at the estuary of the River Ystwyth (this river is pictured *above right*). Aberystwyth is both a holiday resort (dubbed 'The Brighton of Wales') and a university town. The core of the University College of Wales, founded in 1872, is a remarkable neo-Gothic hotel but the main university buildings are situated on the hills overlooking the town. Also to be found here is the National Library of Wales which, along with five other libraries in Britain, shares the privilege of receiving a copy of almost every new book published in this country. Housed in this library is the greatest collection of Welsh books and manuscripts in the world, including copies of the earliest books printed in Welsh. Tenby, another very important Welsh resort, is pictured overleaf.

Tenby is one of the most prosperous resorts in Dyfed, and with its mild climate, golden sands and a harbour (*previous page*) overlooked by colour-washed Georgian houses, it has a character redolent of the Mediterranean. It is situated on a promontory, culminating in a peninsula which is capped by the meagre remains of a castle. This shattered relic, and also the remains of the old walls encircling the town, bear witness to Tenby's earlier importance. Tenby became a walled town in the thirteenth century and in its heyday there were five gateways and about twenty towers. Despite its defences, however, it was twice captured by Parliamentarians during the Civil War, and it has also been twice bombarded from the sea, although its harbour was fortunately well protected. For a time, Tenby was content to remain a moderately prosperous fishing port, but at the start of the nineteenth century the town was remodelled by Sir William Paxton into an elegant watering place which became very fashionable in Victorian times, and has still managed to retain a great deal of its gracious Georgian atmosphere. The marvellous expanse of sands at Tenby have also proved to be a constant asset. There are two completely different shores here: the North Sands, which curve round to the harbour, and the South Sands beyond Castle Hill, yet they are separated by only a few minutes' walk.

In 1957 an area of great beauty, covering over 500 square miles in Powys, was designated the Brecon Beacons National Park. The Brecon Beacons are the highest mountains in South Wales, the loftiest peak being that of Pen-y-Fan at 2,907 feet high. The scenery within the National Park covers mountains and moorlands, forests, limestone foothills and crags cut across by lush river valleys, deep gorges and cascading waterfalls. One such is the Blaen-y-Glyn Falls (*above left*) in the heart of the Tal-y-Bont Forest. Wales is noted for its wonderful cascades, rivers and lakes, but surprisingly enough some of its finest stretches of water are man-made. Lake Vyrnwy (*above*) in Powys is a case in point. Originally the Vyrnwy was just a small stream flowing across marshy lands, but during the 1880s it was converted into a reservoir to provide a water supply for the great city of Liverpool. This reservoir was formed by damming the River Vyrnwy, and the 160-foot-high dam encloses the largest lake in Wales, a sheet of water of over thirty-five square miles, holding 12,131 million gallons. The water is conveyed to Liverpool by an aqueduct seventy-five miles in length, the first two miles of which are tunnelled into the hillside. Fortunately, although the lake is man-made, care has been taken to ensure that it blends perfectly with its beautiful natural surroundings.

Cader Idris is a mountain in Gwynedd, wreathed in mystery and legend. Its name means 'the chair of Idris', who was a mythical giant, but as Idris is the Welsh version of the English name Arthur, it has been suggested that the mountain may even be associated with the tales of King Arthur. The summit of Cader Idris is known as the Craig Lwyd (Sharp Crag) and from this point there is an extensive view over the surrounding countryside, taking in the great sweep of Cardigan Bay and the peaks of Snowdonia. The slopes on the southern flank of Cader Idris are gentle, but those on the northern side are almost perpendicular precipices. At the foot of the mountain is the placid, fish-replete lake of Tal-y-Llyn (*above*) with the tiny Tal-y-Llyn hamlet at its far end. The lake was carved out by ancient glaciers. Lying actually among the crags of Cader Idris is the mysterious lake of Llyn y Cau. This dark and brooding water is reputed to be bottomless, and a monster supposedly lurks in its depths. In the eighteenth century this monster is said to have attacked and killed a boy who was swimming in the lake. Another fascinating legend handed down through the centuries states that anyone who dares to spend the night here will awaken either blind, mad or a poet. In contrast with these grim legends, however, is the ancient belief that Cader Idris is associated with good fairies.

The resort of Barmouth, Gwynedd, stands on the estuary of the Afon Mawddach (*above*), where this river widens after its long journey from a valley beneath Cader Idris, before flowing out into Barmouth Bay. The Barmouth Estuary has been described as 'sublime' – it is spanned by a railway and pedestrian bridge, and it is sometimes said that there is no finer scenery in the whole of Europe than the view of the estuary from this bridge. Further north along the coast is Harlech, which was once a most important town and warranted the protection of a castle. Harlech Castle (*overleaf*) is the southernmost of a chain of castles built to secure Snowdonia during the reign of Edward I. Harlech is a concentric castle with a massive gatehouse, and drum towers set at each corner. It occupies a superb position on a precipitous spur of rock, and once it was guarded by a deep ditch forty feet wide that had been hacked out of the bedrock. In medieval days the sea-level was much higher and a water-gate protected access from the sea. Despite its impregnable appearance, the castle was besieged and taken three times in fifteenth-century wars. Its vulnerability lay in the difficulty of bringing food and supplies to such an isolated garrison and although its defenders fought heroically, they were forced to surrender for want of food and supplies.

The greatest of Edward I's Welsh strongholds, and probably the finest castle in Britain, is the turreted Caernarfon Castle, Gwynedd. Its size alone is impressive, for its outer walls enclose an area of three acres. It was intended to be an impregnable symbol of Plantagenet power in North Wales, but although it succeeded in withstanding an onslaught by Owain Glyndwr in 1401, it fell to the Royalists in the Civil War. Beneath the castle walls lies the town of Caernarfon, centred round its busy market place (*right*). From Caernarfon a road leads inland to the Snowdonia National Forest Park and Snowdon itself; which is the highest mountain in England and Wales. It actually has five peaks and only the loftiest, Y Wyddfa (3,560 feet), qualifies for the title of Snowdon. There are some well-marked tracks to the summit and also a mountain railway. The magnificent Pass of Aberglaslyn (*above*), once described as 'the noblest specimen of the Finely Horrid the Eye can possibly behold', leads from Snowdon towards the village of Beddgelert. Pictured overleaf is the equally magnificent Nant Ffrancon Pass.

The Nant Ffrancon Pass, Gwynedd (its name means the 'Vale of Beavers'), lies in the bed of a glacier (*previous page*), surrounded by great heights, which are a striking example of the wild beauty of the scenery around Snowdon. Carved out from the Snowdon mountain mass are five great cwms, or hollows, with a lake nestling in each, while at the southernmost foot of the mountain is Llyn Gwynant (*above*), set in pastoral surroundings. Near the hamlet of Capel Garmon (*below right*) is a fine cromlech, or burial chamber, which probably dates from the Bronze Age. It is enclosed by a dry-stone wall and comprises a triple chamber. A few miles away is Betws-y-Coed, claimed to be 'the beauty spot of Wales'. There are three lovely waterfalls here, but the best known are the Swallow Falls on the River Llugwy. The island at Anglesey (also known as Môn – the mother of Wales) is separated from the mainland by the Menai Strait. On Anglesey, guarding the eastern entrance to the Strait, is Beaumaris Castle (*above right*). This is a perfect example of a concentric castle with inner and outer baileys and great drum towers protecting the eight-sided outer wall. The castle is surrounded by a moat, which was once connected to the sea by a canal. Building was begun by Edward I in 1295, and 400 masons and 2,000 labourers were engaged at a cost of about £250 a day (a vast amount of money in the Middle Ages). Its walls are thick enough to contain a passage within them. To the south of the castle is the village of Llanfairpwllgwyngyllgogerychwyrndrobwll-llantysiliogogogoch, justly famous for having the longest name in Britain. Here there is a delightful little church with an ancient font.

The greatest river of North Wales is the Dee, which is some seventy miles in length and flows through Lake Bala in Gwynedd on its way to the Irish Sea. Lake Bala is the largest natural lake in Wales, being half a mile wide and over four miles long. Its Welsh name is Lleyn Tegid. It is a popular lake for sailing and fishing and it does contain one species of fish, the gwyniad, which is peculiar to itself and can be found nowhere else. Several legends are attached to Lake Bala, including a story of a drowned palace beneath the waters, and an old belief that the River Dee flowed through the lake without their waters mingling. From Bala, the Dee flows down to Llangollen, Clwyd, and here the scenery of the river valley is particularly lovely (*above*). On the banks of the Dee about ten miles from Llangollen is Corwen, one of the principal venues of Eisteddfods in Wales.

The village of Llanrhaedyr-ym-Mochnant, Powys (*above*) takes its name from the Pistyll Rhaeadr Falls where the water of the Disgynfa falls over 200 feet down the hillside in a succession of torrents. This is probably the finest waterfall in Wales and George Borrow wrote of it: 'I never saw water falling so gracefully, so much like thin beautiful threads as here.' Although the falls are the greatest attraction, the village itself contains many features of interest, such as the church. This church has no saint's name but is called instead the 'Church by the Falls of the Swift Brook'. Inside is a rare Celtic cross slab. In 1540 William Morgan was born in the village. It was he who translated the Bible into Welsh and laid the foundations for the modern forms of the Welsh language. Henry VIII had banned the official use of this language, but Elizabeth I lifted the ban in 1567.

SCOTLAND

The land of the lonely bagpiper playing his pipes on the top of a mountain watched by the Monarch of the Glen is the romantic notion of Scotland fostered by Queen Victoria, sundry poets and artists, and subsequent generations of public relations men. This is an appealing message, and there is more than a germ of truth in it, like the Scottish Tourist Board photograph that showed a deserted Highland road snaking across the moors with the caption – 'The Applecross Rush Hour, 9 a.m.'. Certainly there is no difficulty in getting away from people in Scotland, for in comparison with England it is a big, under-populated country. Those who are prepared to leave their cars and walk to viewpoints or the less-accessible beauty-spots will often not meet a soul on their excursions. This is in marked contrast to the major tourist roads which are busy all through the summer.

It is the sheer size of Scotland that amazes many people. It is over 360 miles from Dumfries to John o' Groats – a fair day's drive. The awkward corners and appendages of the country also make for long journeys. By road it is 134 miles from Glasgow to Campbeltown, though a crow would fly half of that distance. Many of Scotland's offshore islands lie a long way from the mainland (altogether there are 787 islands off the coast of Scotland, 136 of them inhabited). For example, the Shetland Islands are 186 miles from Aberdeen, a fact that makes the miracle of the offshore oilfield even more remarkable.

Scotland has only a handful of cities but she is compensated by her smaller towns, of which there is an abundance, most notably in the south. Moffat, for example, is a place typical of these, with a large market-place surrounded by handsome buildings; altogether a very functional place of banks, shops and hotels with the usual attorneys' and land agents' offices interspersed. The latter have intriguing pictures in the windows of baronial mansions currently on the market, and notices announcing forthcoming sales of cottage furniture or livestock. To capture the real flavour of such a town it is best to attend one of these sales – you never know, you might end up owning fishing rights on one of the finest salmon rivers!

As one moves northwards the character of the towns changes. In the industrial central valley many are obviously dependent on their steelworks or coal mines. To the north they again assume the more leisurely mantle of country towns. Tourism plays an important part in the lives of people here, and many of the shops that would formerly have sold hardware or harness to the hill-farmers now stock craft-work and other 'ethnic' souvenirs. Towns such as Fort William and Braemar are very well geared to provide for every need of the tourist (one of Britain's most luxurious hotels is situated close to Fort William), while those on the east coast (unjustly neglected by the tourist) are left in a romantic state of neglect – at least as far as the holiday traveller is concerned. Fortunately the oil boom has revived the fortunes of many of these small seaside fishing towns.

In the remote regions of the north-west it would at first appear that the hand of man has lain lightly on the landscape of mountain, moor and water. It is strange to think today that once much of this area was a forest, which finally vanished when sheep were introduced between 1750 and 1850. Today this countryside is lonely but once it was comparatively densely populated, occupied by crofters who lived in the cottages whose bare skeletons still show today. They scraped a living from these forbidding lands until the Risings of the eighteenth century. Then many of the Scottish landlords were dispossessed (or killed at Culloden). Their estates were given to English supporters of the Hanoverian regime, the government being keen to suppress the clan system and discourage the 'auld religion'. It was the new landlords, most of whom continued to live in England, who introduced sheep, driving crofters off their lands to make way for them. This form of 'clearance' was not confined to the Highlands of Scotland but also took place in England, where the name for it was 'enclosure' (the erection of fences around the common land to keep the sheep in, the people and their cattle out). In both countries the result was the same. A great exodus of country people to the new lands beyond the seas where a man could make a living for himself by traditional means. Thus the bravest independent spirits fled to Canada, America and Australia. It is ironic that the end of the Clearances (between 1840 and 1880) coincided with Queen Victoria's enthusiasm for Scotland which led to the re-introduction of the tartan and Highland customs which had been banned by her predecessors.

The pageantry of Highland life remains popular to this day. The great event of the year is the Braemar Gathering which, appropriately, takes place close to Queen Victoria's Scottish residence, Balmoral Castle. Here the crowds come to watch the dancing, pipe-playing and caber-tossing that are highlights of similar events staged all over Scotland in the summer. In the Lowlands the Edinburgh Festival holds pride of place. This international festival of music and drama attracts thousands of people to the Scottish capital each year. Unofficial productions 'beyond the fringe' of the proper festival put on by obscure companies are often acclaimed with great enthusiasm and go on to be successes in London and elsewhere. The famous Tattoo, held on the parade-ground with the Castle as a dramatic backdrop, is a great feature of the fortnight.

Situated on a rugged, precipitous outcrop of volcanic rock, with battlements silhouetted against the western skies, Edinburgh Castle (*previous page*) reigns majestic and serene, the emblem of Edinburgh. Within its walls, which have heard so many dark secrets of treachery and romance, lies the foundation stone of all Edinburgh; Saint Margaret's Chapel. This was built in about 1090, by Queen Margaret, who brought the Roman form of Christianity into Scotland. The famous ruin of Tantallon Castle (*top left*) stands, still triumphant, in its superb position on the craggy coastline, opposite the Bass Rock. It features a curtain wall which is twelve feet thick. Embedded in the austere walls of this fourteenth-century Douglas stronghold, is the essence of Scotland. It withstood many a siege until it was dismantled by General Monk, in 1651. The palatial Floors Castle (*left*), seat of the Duke of Roxburgh, stands just outside Kelso in its extensive park, bordered by the River Tweed. The castle was originally designed by Vanbrugh for the first Duke in 1718, but was later altered by Playfair, and shows Tudor-style work. In Roxburgh Street, Kelso, are the 'golden gates', leading to the castle drive. Erected in 1929, they feature ornate wrought-iron work overlaid with gold leaf. Mellerstain (*above*) is a distinguished eighteenth-century mansion, designed by William and Robert Adam. Owned by the Earl of Haddington, Mellerstain lies near Kelso, and is one of the finest Georgian houses Scotland possesses. The library, which is one of Adam's masterpieces, includes a splendid frieze, and the ceiling has an affinity with a piece of Wedgwood porcelain. Terraced gardens gently slope down from the house to an ornamental lake.

Saint Mary's Loch (*previous page*), set in the green, flowing Lowland hills in Ettrick Forest, Selkirkshire, is indeed a beautiful and tranquil scene. Its charms have been recognised, both by Wordsworth, in his *Yarrow Visited*, and by Scott, in *Marmion*. Traquair House (*top left*) is among the finest of the early Scottish mansions, and is claimed to be one of the oldest inhabited houses in the country. At one time it was the home of William the Lion, who held court here in 1209. The main gateway is guarded by two stone bears, the original Veolan in Scott's *Waverly*. The gates have been closed since the seventh Countess of Traquair died in 1786, although tradition says that they were closed in 1745, not to be re-opened until a Stuart ascended the throne again. Caerlaverock Castle (*left*), once a great triangular structure, is an impressive ruin now. It is moated and has towers at each corner, and a double-towered gatehouse. The castle, probably built in about 1290, was formerly a Maxwell stronghold, whose crest appears over the principal entrance. It has had a turbulent history of sieges, notably of Edward I in 1300, and by the Covenanters in 1640. Too often the Highlands take precedence over beautiful landscapes like this one in Kirkcudbrightshire (*above*). The ruined border keep is Orchardton Tower, which stands a mile south of Palnackie. The circular tower is late fifteenth century, and was built originally by John Cairns.

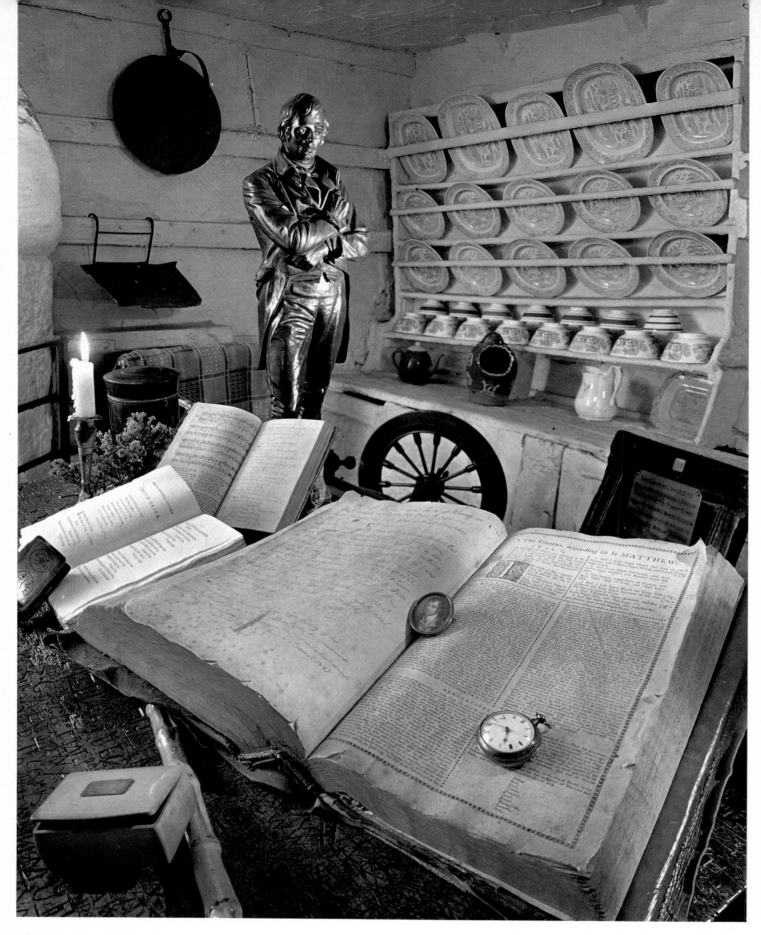

The photograph *above* depicts a kitchen scene at the birthplace of Robert Burns in Alloway. Shown on the kitchen table are exhibits from the museum, including Burns's snuff-box, his walking stick, and his family Bible; also the Kilmarnock edition of his poems and a manuscript of 'Auld Lang Syne'. This idyllic evening scene (*above right*) shows the sun setting behind the Cowal hills. This hilly region is punctuated by several picturesque sea lochs. Here, over one of them, the last glimpse of the warm evening sun with its reflection on the wind-ruffled water is recorded for posterity. Rothesay Castle (*right*) is one of the most remarkable medieval castles in Scotland. It was built in about 1098, during the Norse occupation, but since that time it has been the victim of various styles of architecture, passed through many hands, and braved many sieges, notably that of Cromwell in the seventeenth century, when it was largely destroyed. It is an excellent illustration of a thirteenth-century castle; with high curtain walls enclosing a circular courtyard. This is a unique design in Scotland. The whole structure is surrounded by a deep moat, and the entrance is through an eminent tower that stands out into the moat; it is this tower that is the work of James IV and James V.

Glencoe (*previous page*) is unquestionably the most famous pass in Scotland. In Gaelic it is named the 'Glen of Weeping', because of its sober historical associations. For this is the site of the violent and cold-blooded Glencoe massacre in 1692 when the Campbells and Government troops killed over forty of the Macdonald Clan (with whom they had lived amicably for twelve days), under the orders of William III. All because their Chief was a few days late in taking the oath of allegiance to the King. The River Coe wends its way along the bottom of the stony glen, with the wild and haunting mountainside towering above, as if commanding its submission. Some 13,000 acres of Glencoe, including the site of the massacre, have been the property of The National Trust for Scotland since 1937.

The Isle of Mull is the largest of the Inner Hebrides, although it is only about thirty miles long. But its craggy coastline, due to numerous sea lochs and indentations that cut into the land, consequently measures about 300 miles. Tobermory is the main centre. Originally founded as a fishing village in 1788, it occupies a dramatic position in an islet-sheltered spot in the north-east. At one point the island is almost severed; opposite the Sound of Mull, where the inlet of Loch na Keal (*above*), on the western coast, is separated from the Sound by only three miles of land. Farming and forestry on a very limited scale is all that this island is able to cope with, as the land is very wild, although it is ideal for quite a number of private estates which are devoted to sport, including deer, grouse and fish. But this attractive isle has plenty to offer the person who is in love with the open-air life and beautiful scenery. Narrow, meandering roads wend their way through the lush wilderness of the island. Ben More, the highest mountain at 3,169 feet, stands quietly surveying the isle. Considering the size of the Isle of Mull, there are quite a number of old castles. This is the result of the military enthusiasm of Mullmen in former times. The castles were christened with names such as Glengorm, and Torosay. Two particularly fine ruined castles, Aros and Duart, were restored in 1912 by the Chief of the Maclean Clan. At one time the Macleans were almost the sole inhabitants of the Isle of Mull, but many of the Island's men were lost during the Napoleonic Wars.

The romantic ruins of Kilchurn Castle (*above*) stand at the north-east end of Loch Awe, on a rock which was, at one time, an island but is now enclosed by marshland. This charming old castle dates originally from the year 1440. It was a stronghold of the Campbell Clan, and Sir Colin Campbell of Glenorchy, founder of the Breadalbane family, built the Keep. The south side was built in the sixteenth century, but the north side was not completed until the seventeenth century. The Campbells, whose views were anti-Jacobite in the eighteenth century, offered the use of the castle to the Hanoverian troops for a garrison in 1746. The disastrous gale of 1879, which wrecked the Tay Bridge, also blew down one of the tops of the castle's towers. However, the castle, in its position of remarkable beauty, remains one of the finest baronial ruins in Scotland.

And as the shadows grow longer on the clear blue water, and the mist makes its way down into the valley, and begins to swirl around the ruined towers, it is a difficult task to reject the atmosphere of the past which imposes itself upon us. Indeed, Scotland has quite an amount of beauty to offer; having been richly endowed with both stern and romantic castles, serene and stately houses, not forgetting great natural beauty, all portrayed on a rich, historical backcloth. The turbulent Scotland of the olden days has left a legacy to modern-day Scotland which cannot be ignored.

Previous page: Castle Tioram on Loch Moidart, built on a rocky outcrop connected to the mainland by a sandy causeway, is a castle that seems to have stepped straight from a fairy-tale. Parts of it date from the early thirteenth century, though substantial additions were made about 1600. It was the home of the Macdonalds of Clanranald, and was left ruinous by the head of the Clan when he went to join the Jacobite forces in 1715. Sir Walter Scott would have loved this romantic place, just as he was inspired by the rugged scenery of the Trossachs (*above*), which is centred on beautiful Loch Katrine. To the north is the village of Killin (*opposite*), where the waters of the River Dochart tumble into Loch Tay after a night of heavy rain. *Overleaf:* the Glenfinnan Monument stands at the head of Loch Shiel. It is a memorial to the Highlanders who fought for Prince Charles Edward Stuart in the Rising of 1745.

The Isle of Skye is easily reached from the mainland by way of a short ferry trip from Kyle of Lochalsh. Everything about the island is magical. Its 'winged shape' on the map looks as though it is leaping off into the Atlantic. Its rugged mountains provide some of the best rock climbing to be found in Scotland. The famous Cuillins range has summits that were only conquered at the end of the last century. Blaven, 3,042 feet, to the east of the Cuillins, is shown from the village of Torrin, on Loch Slapin (*picture on previous page*). The black rock faces of Blaven give climbers difficult ascents, particularly by the notorious Clach Glas ridge. Sea lochs bite deep into the interior of Skye, and in many places the old ways of crofting survive: the people living from sheep and fishing. Peat smoke rests heavy on the air and Sunday remains a day for peace and reflection (until recently there were no Sunday ferries). The mountains of Torridon (of red sandstone, some distinctively capped with white quartzite) are also favourites with climbers. The jagged peaks are linked by narrow, exciting ridges which make wonderful viewpoints, the vistas extending from Cape Wrath, the Ardnamurchan peninsula, Skye and beyond, to the distant islands of the Outer Hebrides. One of the mountains overlooking Glen Torridon (*opposite page*) is Ben Eighe (3,188 feet) which has a National Nature Reserve embracing 10,000 acres, the haunt of the wild cat and golden eagle. The Outer Hebrides lack the accessibility of Skye; all of them entail a lengthy sea crossing ranging from two and a half to six or more hours. However, the effort of getting there is worthwhile. Although both Harris and Lewis are called islands, in fact they are joined. On the latter island is the stone circle of Callanish (*below*). This dates from the Bronze Age (300–1500 BC) and is one of four stone circles put up within a four-mile radius of Callanish. Its significance remains an enigma – there are countless theories of astronomy and astrology to explain its purpose, yet essentially this remains a place of mystery – entirely appropriate in these islands of other-worldy beauty. Harris has a more mountainous landscape than that of Lewis, with its highest peak being that of Clisham at 2,622 feet, but both islands have spectacular beaches of silver sand, only frequented by holidaymakers in the height of summer: during the rest of the year they are left to the gulls, the cattle and the sheep.

Because of its wonderful situation on Loch Duich, Eilean Donan Castle (*previous page*) is photographed more than any other Scottish castle. As its name implies, it was once completely secure on its islet, about 100 yards off the shore. Later a causeway was built to improve access. Headquarters of the Clan Macrae, the castle is close to Dornie on the 'Road to the Isles' from Inverness to Kyle of Lochalsh. The coast of north-west Scotland has a type of wild beauty unknown elsewhere in Britain. Once much of the area was covered in forest, but this disappeared between 1550 and 1770 so that now the landscape is left bare and forbidding, yet with its mountains, myriads of lochs and lochans, and wonderful coastline, it weaves a strange spell over the visitor. A tortuous road follows the coast northwards, passing through the village of Drumbeg, near to which this picture of Loch Achaipn Bhan (*below*) was taken. Such lochs are famous for the trout that they produce. To the north again is the village of Durness – also surrounded by many lochans, some of which have limestone bottoms, which encourage colonies of freshwater shrimps, a favourite diet of trout which even outdo those of Drumbeg in quantity and quality. Cape Wrath (aptly named) on the far side of the Kyle, is Scotland's north-western extremity. It can be reached by ferry and Land Rover (or on foot). There are many fine beaches around Durness (like the one shown *opposite*). On the other corner of Scotland's northern coastline is John o' Groats and fractionally even further to the north are the awesome cliffs of Duncansby Head (*opposite, below*).

The great Norman cathedral at Kirkwall, the 'capital' of the Orkney Islands, is one that many a mainland city would be proud to call its own. In fact, the only other pre-Reformation Scottish cathedral to survive intact is St Mungo's, Glasgow. The rich colour of its interior stonework makes St Magnus's Cathedral memorable, and the effect is heightened by the massive piers of the nave (*above*), dating from the twelfth century when stonemasons in the south were already beginning to build lighter, graceful supports. The cathedral was erected by a pagan nephew of Magnus, a Norse chieftain renowned for his goodness, who was murdered. It was intended as a tribute to his saintly virtues, and both he and his nephew (who was later converted) are buried side by side in their magnificent cathedral. Aviemore, at the heart of Scotland's central massif, the Cairngorm range, has in the last twenty years become one of Britain's premier resorts. Previously it was a remote Highland village on the main road to the north between Perth and Inverness. Today it is the leading winter sports centre, with every facility available, and in the summer too it attracts tourists and sportsmen. The large hotels even have a thriving conference business. The mountain scenery here is truly magnificent, one of its features being the numerous small lochs, such as Loch Insh (*top, opposite*), set amid the pine forests. Portknockie (*opposite, below*) is one of many fishing ports.

The River Dee, the fifth longest river in Scotland, has its source near the summit of Braeriach, some 4,000 feet above sea-level at the heart of the Cairngorms. It flows a long way before entering that part of its course known as Royal Deeside, by the royal deer forests of Ballochbuie, Balmoral and Glengairn. Before Queen Victoria 'took up' this part of the world a road led into the first of these forests, being carried over the Dee by the 'Old Bridge' (*above opposite*). The Prince Consort re-routed the road and closed the bridge, leaving it to become a picturesque ruin. It was built in 1752. Immediately upstream from Braemar the Dee is at its most beautiful. Mountains, trees and rushing water join together to present an unforgettable natural spectacle. Braemar has become a popular resort with tourists. Once it was a favourite residence of the Kings of Scotland who came here for the hunting. A 'hunting party' invited by the Earl of Mar met here on 26 August 1715. Its members organised the first Jacobite Rising. An Earl of Mar built Braemar Castle (*opposite*) in 1628, though in 1689 it was burnt down to prevent it from falling into the hands of the Hanoverians. However, the latter rebuilt it and it survives today as a rare example of a fortress of this period. Dunnotar Castle (*above*) is situated on the east coast two miles south of Stonehaven. This site was fortified from early times, though the parts of the ruin still standing so impressively today date from the fourteenth century with considerable additions being made two centuries later.

Glen Clova (*above*) strikes deep into the heart of the central massif from the south-east. Hardy walkers can struggle over the watershed to reach Braemar or Ballater. From the summit of these paths there are breathtaking views to the peaks of the Cairngorms and, later, to Deeside. Glen Clova is famous botanically for its flora, especially alpines, and its mosses. Culross, on the northern shore of the Firth of Forth, is an essential venue for anyone interested in Scottish architecture. It was a busy little port in the late sixteenth and early seventeenth centuries, but later lost its trade and fell into neglect. Thus a great many of its early buildings survive (*above opposite*), and some are in the care of the National Trust for Scotland. These and its cobbled streets make the town a showplace of the Central Lowlands. Pittenweem is on the coast of Fife, at the mouth of the Firth. Like Culross its harbour (*opposite*) is an ancient one, the Royal Burgh being granted its charter in 1542 by James V, thus consolidating the fortunes of the town that had grown up around the Priory founded in the twelfth century. The parish church, dating from the end of the sixteenth century, has a tower more befitting to a castle than a church. This is not the only picturesque feature of the place: it has delightful old fishermen's houses lining narrow wynds that lead down to the harbour. This has led to popularity with artists and its soubriquet – 'the St Ives of Scotland'. Castle Campbell (*overleaf*) is near Dollar, also to the north of the Firth. The Earl of Argyll built it in the latter years of the fifteenth century though much was added later. It was left a ruin by Montrose in 1645. The castle's situation is one of the most romantic in Scotland, for the glen in which it stands is surrounded by deep ravines.

There are striking parallels between Stirling (*above*) and Edinburgh. Both utilise the sites of long-dead volcanoes as defensive positions, but whereas the former is only the 'Gateway to the Highlands', the latter was always the country's capital. After an uneasy history up to the early fifteenth century, Stirling became established as a seat of the Stuart monarchs. Like Edinburgh it has its Old Town around the Castle, and a New Town of the nineteenth century below, towards the station. Linlithgow Palace was another favourite residence of the Stuarts; begun by James I (of Scotland) it was completed by James V. His daughter, Mary Queen of Scots, was born here in 1542. The Palace was burnt down, perhaps accidentally, by Government troops in 1746. The unusual Cross Well (*below*) dates from 1807.

INDEX OF ILLUSTRATIONS

SBN 85306 868 2
First published 1980
© 1980 Jarrold and Sons Ltd, Norwich. This book is produced by Jarrold Colour Publications, Norwich, in conjunction with the British Tourist Authority. Illustration material from the B.T.A. photographic library and the picture library of Jarrold Colour Publications. Photographs of Caerlaverock Castle and the Callanish Standing Stones are British Crown Copyright: reproduced by kind permission of the Scottish Development Department. The photograph of Stonehenge is Crown Copyright: reproduced by kind permission of the Controller of Her Majesty's Stationery Office.
Printed and bound in Great Britain by Jarrold and Sons Ltd, Norwich, England.